SCO

October 23–N ber 21

You cannot shake hands with a clenched fist.

Indira Gandhi

GERANIUM

Scorpio
I am a
LOVER
and a
FIGHTER

autumn

Never
Underestimate
a Scorpio

Scorpio
Ruled by Mars and Pluto

Scorpio

Confident

PASSIONATE

DETERMINED

FIERCE

Instinctive

RULING HOUSE
8
The House of Rebirth

SCORPIO

My vulnerability is my strength

Images by Andrea Lauren © Simon & Schuster, Inc., and 123RF/Volodymyr Horbovyy

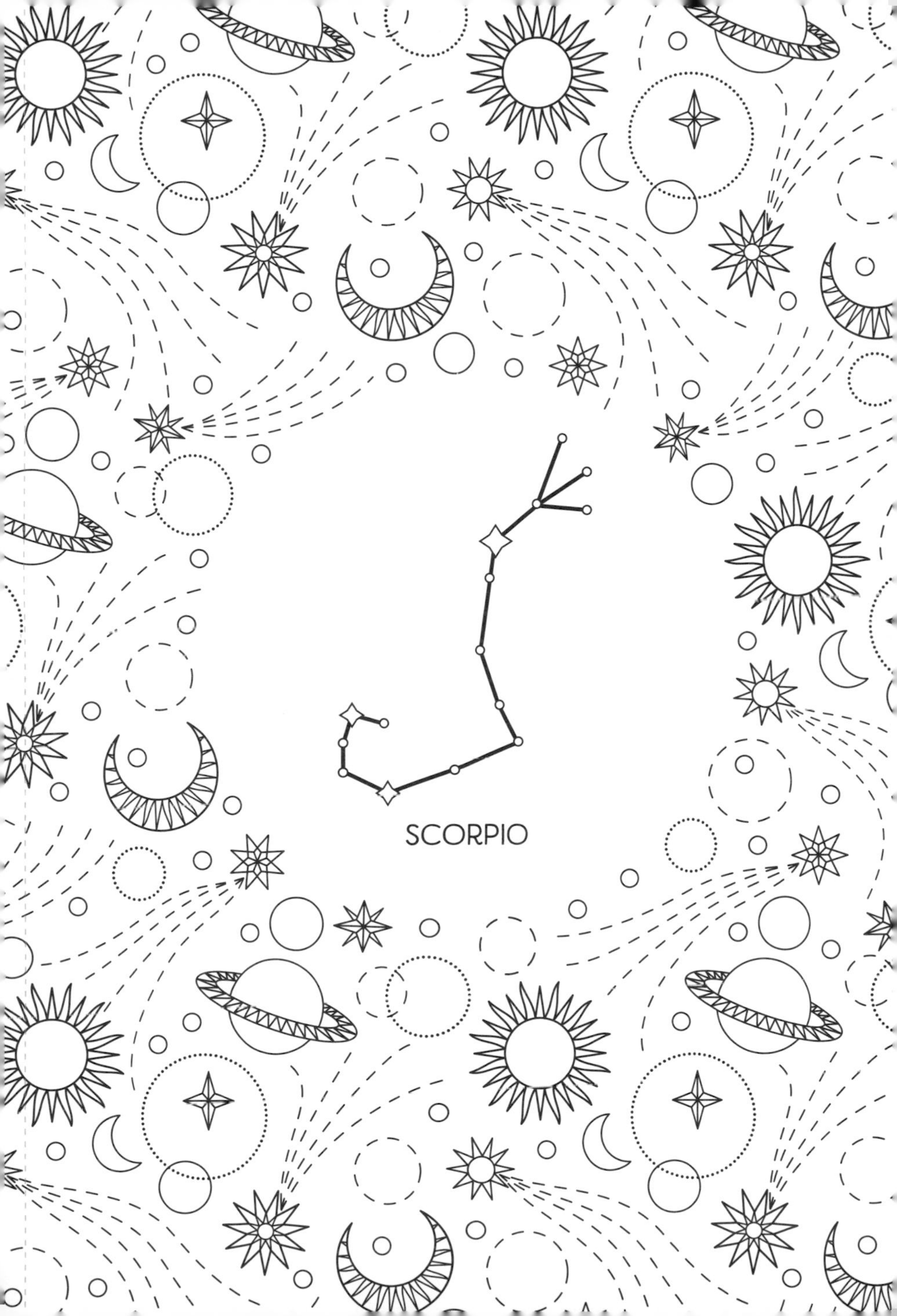
SCORPIO

Aries
Taurus
Gemini
Cancer
Leo
Virgo
Libra
Scorpio
Sagittarius
Capricorn
Aquarius
Pisces

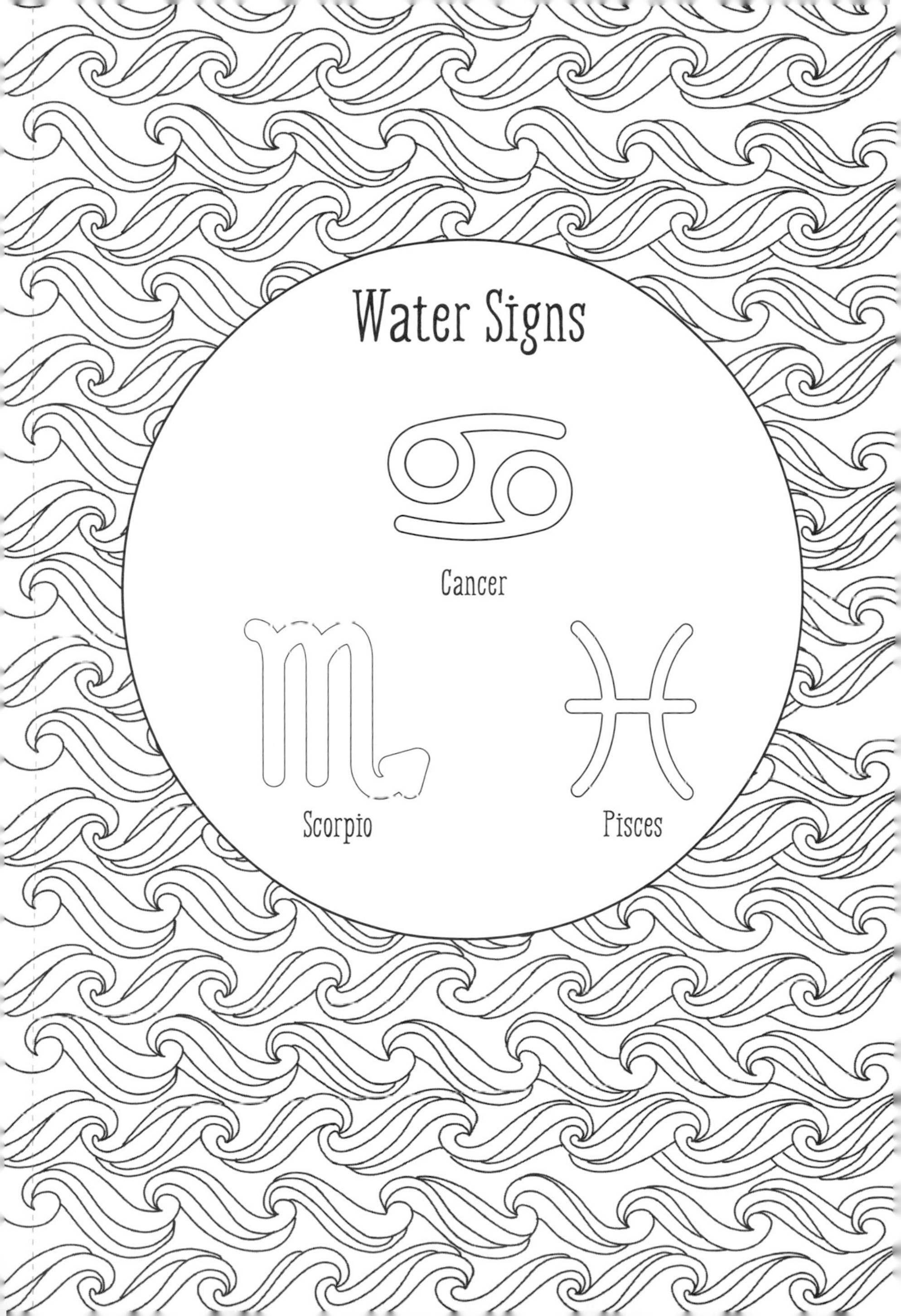
Water Signs
Cancer
Scorpio
Pisces

LET THE STARS LEAD THE WAY

Image by Andrea Lauren © Simon & Schuster, Inc.